Colored pencil and marker art by Joan Janse.

Colored pencil and marker art by Leah Honarbakhsh.

Crayon art by Christine Belleris.

Colored pencil and marker art by Lawna Patterson Oldfield.

Nature is painting for us,
day after day,
pictures of infinite beauty.

—JOHN RUSHKIN

NATURE PROVIDES A DAZZLING ARRAY OF COLORS in the animal kingdom—the bold stripes of a tiger, a tapestry of teals in a peacock's feathers, or the rainbow of colors in a toucan. While most of us are far removed from wild animals in our everyday lives, we can celebrate their majesty by adding our own burst of colors to the menagerie of animals in this book. Paired with inspiring quotes of lessons that we humans can learn from our animal counterparts, we hope this book inspires you to unplug, unwind, and unleash your inner artist.

WHY COLOR? Yes, believe it or not, scientists have studied coloring, and they've found that it quiets the mind, calms our thoughts, and reduces stress. Coloring can induce a kind of "flow," or active meditation, during which you lose your sense of time and your worries fade away. So grab your favorite pencils or markers and let your imagination and creativity take flight.

Tips to Make Your Pages Come to Life

COLORING IS MEANT TO BE A STRESS-FREE, no-worries activity. There really is no right or wrong way to do it. But for anyone who wants to take it to another level, here are some tips:

STIPPLING—*Stippling* is a good way to add texture to your art. Stippling means to place many tiny dots on the surface. Your dots can be close together or far apart, depending upon the effect you are trying to create (you can stipple trees, water, flowers, or the sky—anything really!).

HATCHING—*Hatching* is when you draw a series of parallel lines in the same direction.

CROSS-HATCHING—As the name implies, *cross-hatching* means that you draw a series of parallel lines and then you make another set of parallel lines in another direction on top of the first set of lines. This creates both shading and texture.

BASIC SHADING—Use two similar colors to create a dimensional shading effect. Choose one lighter color and one darker color, both in the same color family. Leave the darker area with one color and then blend the colors together to create the lighter shade. Blending the strokes together will add depth and dimension.

Basic stroke

Stippling

Hatching

Cross-hatching

BLENDING COLORS—By blending several colors together, you can create a three-dimensional shading effect. For example, if you want to color a leaf green, use the color wheel on the next page to choose several shades of green as well as some colors next to the green (yellows and blues). Try to envision where the light would be falling on your image. Wherever the light would fall on the leaf is where you will place your lightest colors (the lighter greens and yellow). Wherever the shadow would fall is where you would place your darker colors (the darker green and a bit of blue). By overlapping the colors and blending them, you will create a realistic effect. It helps to practice on a piece of scrap paper first, and to work slowly to see if you are creating the effect you wish before you complete a large area.

COLORING THE DETAILS—You'll notice each design is made up of unique doodled designs. You can color each individual element on its own in a separate color or you can fill in one larger group of shapes in one color.

Shading with different tones

A Note from the Illustrator

THANK YOU SO MUCH FOR ALLOWING MY ART to come into your life. I am honored to share my illustrations with you. As an illustrator, my vision is to combine beauty from nature and my imagination to create hand-drawn images that inspire others. I hope that the quotes inspire you to live life to its fullest and I hope that the illustrations inspire you to unleash your creativity. The best thing about art is there are no rules, and this book is full of endless coloring possibilities. The only thing that I ask you to do is to have fun. So turn the page, get started, and let your creativity flow!

Best wishes, *Anna N. Carey*

ANNA N. CAREY *is a dog lover, art teacher, and freelance artist. She resides in Columbia, Missouri, with her husband and two dogs, Paisley and Hazel. To see more of her art, you can follow her on Instagram @PaisleyandHazel.*

Coloring Tools

TIP: Add a piece of scrap paper under each page you're working on to make sure that the ink doesn't bleed through the page.

COLORED PENCILS: great for shading or blending colors together, both of which add interest and depth to any design.

GEL PENS AND MARKERS: good for adding bold, defined bursts of color.

CRAYONS: surprisingly versatile when filling in large spaces.

Choose Your Colors

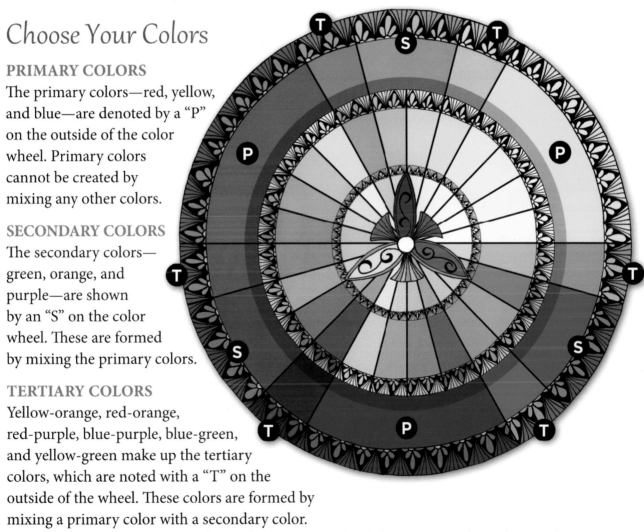

PRIMARY COLORS

The primary colors—red, yellow, and blue—are denoted by a "P" on the outside of the color wheel. Primary colors cannot be created by mixing any other colors.

SECONDARY COLORS

The secondary colors—green, orange, and purple—are shown by an "S" on the color wheel. These are formed by mixing the primary colors.

TERTIARY COLORS

Yellow-orange, red-orange, red-purple, blue-purple, blue-green, and yellow-green make up the tertiary colors, which are noted with a "T" on the outside of the wheel. These colors are formed by mixing a primary color with a secondary color.

The colors on the top half of the wheel are considered the warmer colors whereas the bottom hues are the cooler ones. Colors that fall opposite of one another on the wheel are complementary, and the ones that fall next to each other are analogous. You can use both complementary and analogous colors to make a gorgeous piece of art—the possibilities are as endless as your imagination.

Harmony How-Tos

JUST AS IN LIFE, BALANCE IS THE KEY to creating harmony in any relationship—even when coloring. You can find a rainbow of inspiration all around you—in the patterns of plants, animals, flowers, sunsets, and even the morning sky.

A nature-inspired color scheme with analogous colors

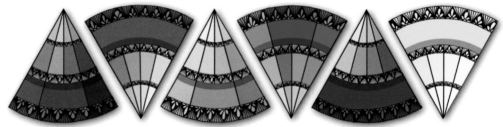

ANALOGOUS COLORS are any three colors which are side by side on a 12-part color wheel, such as yellow-green, yellow, and yellow-orange or teal blue, blue, and indigo.

A nature-inspired color scheme with complementary colors

COMPLEMENTARY COLORS are any two colors which are directly opposite each other, such as yellow and purple or orange and blue.

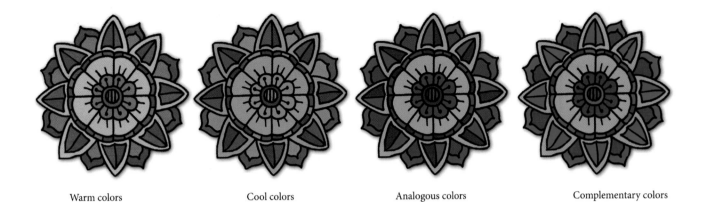

Warm colors   Cool colors   Analogous colors   Complementary colors

Pick Your Palette:

Having a hard time picking your palette? Don't worry. Try some of these combinations. You can find many resources online or by looking at the colors in nature. You can work with one color family or a few.

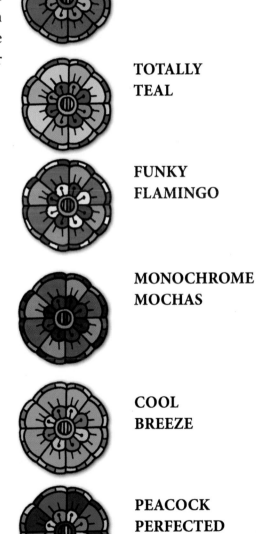

COTTON CANDY APPLE

TOTALLY TEAL

FUNKY FLAMINGO

MONOCHROME MOCHAS

COOL BREEZE

PEACOCK PERFECTED

Use the following colored pages as your inspiration. Happy coloring!

Colored pencil art by Ted Janse.

Colored pencil and marker art by Lawna Patterson Oldfield.

Colored digital art by Larissa Hise Henoch.

Colored marker art by Kim Weiss.

Be a flamingo in a flock of pigeons.

—AUTHOR UNKNOWN

Love makes the wildest spirit tame,

and the tamest spirit wild.

—ALEXIS DELP

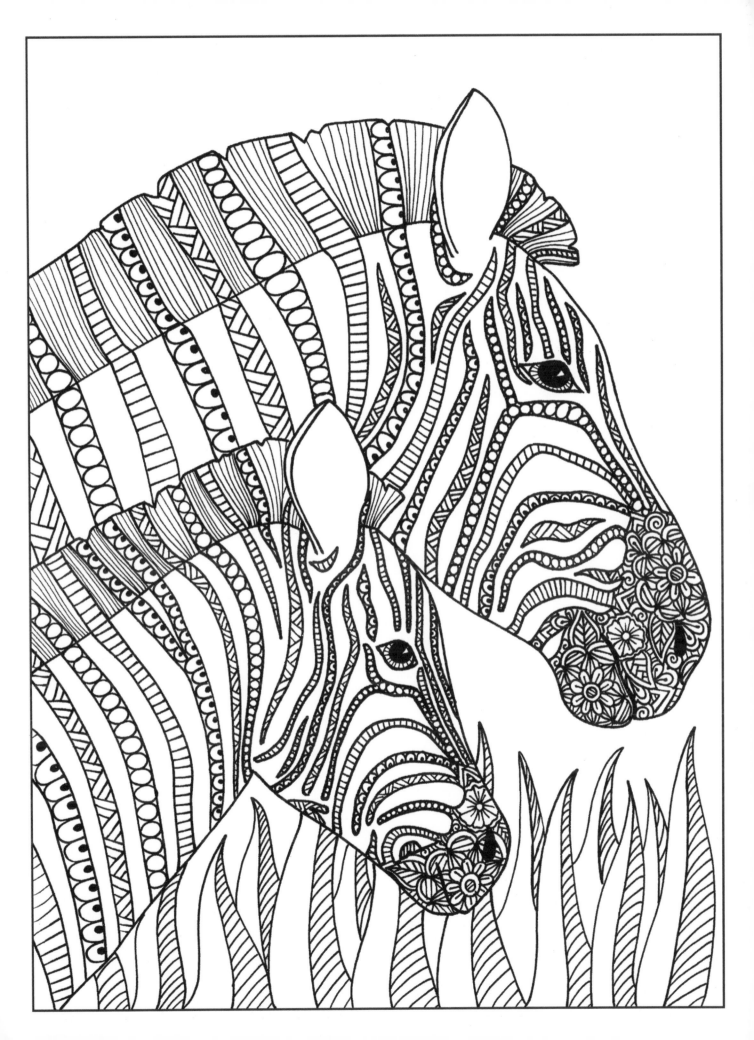

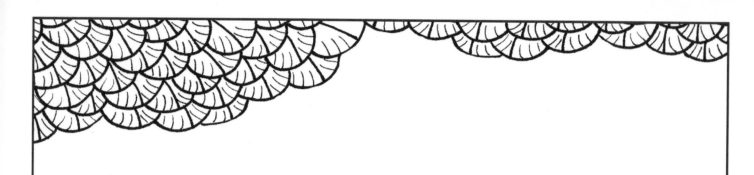

People are crying up the rich and variegated
plumage of the peacock, and he is himself
blushing at the sight of his ugly feet.

—SAADI

When you are a giraffe and you receive criticism from turtles, they are reporting the view from the level they are on.

—TD JAKES

Look deep into nature and then you will

understand everything better.

—ALBERT EINSTEIN

The earth has music for those who listen.

—GEORGE SANTAYANA

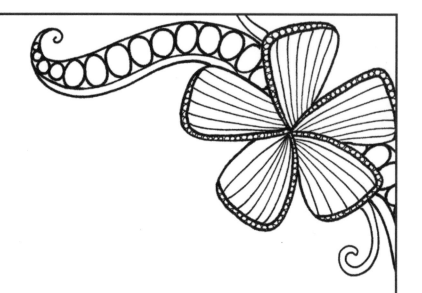

Only those who risk going too far

can possibly find out how

far one can go.

—T.S. ELIOT

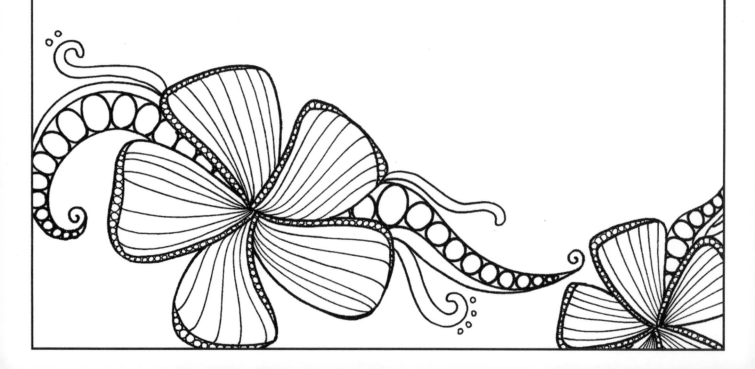

Nature always wears the colors

of the spirit.

—RALPH WALDO EMERSON

Nature does not hurry,

yet everything is accomplished.

—LAO TZU

It is not only fine feathers

that make fine birds.

—AESOP

Love is a chain of love

as nature is a chain of life.

—TRUMAN CAPOTE

A tiger does not shout its tigritude; it acts.

—WOLE SOYINKA

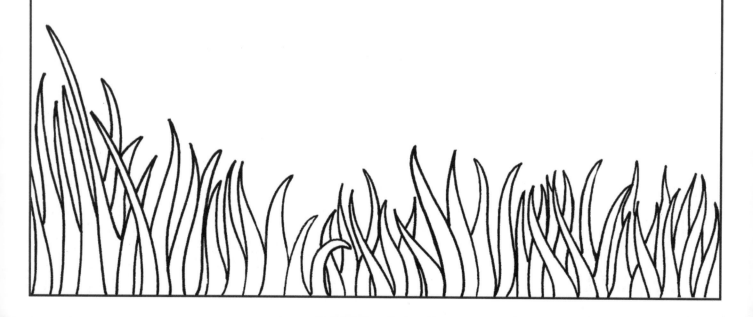

The butterfly counts not months

but moments, and has time enough.

—RABINDRANATH TAGORE

I call horses "divine mirrors"—

they reflect back the emotions you put in.

If you put in love and respect and kindness and

curiosity, the horse will return that.

—ALLAN HAMILTON

Animals share with us the privilege

of having a soul.

—PYTHAGORAS

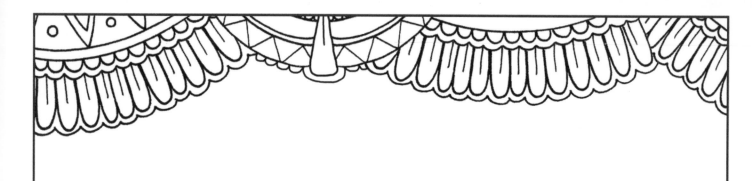

It is better to live one day as a lion,

than a thousand days as a lamb.

—ROMAN PROVERB

Happiness often sneaks in
through a door you didn't know
you left open.

—JOHN BARRYMORE

One touch of nature makes the

whole world kin.

—WILLIAM SHAKESPEARE

The fox has many tricks.

The hedgehog has but one.

But that is the best of all.

—RALPH WALDO EMERSON

With foxes we must play the fox.

—THOMAS FULLER

An owl is the wisest of all birds

because the more it sees, the less it talks.

—CHRISTIE WATSON

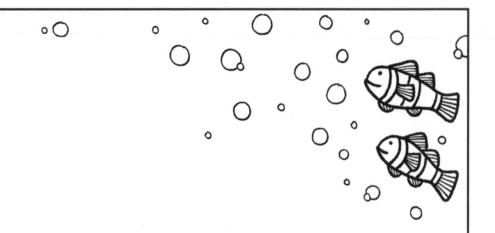

You must live in the present,

launch yourself on every wave, find your

eternity in each moment.

—HENRY DAVID THOREAU

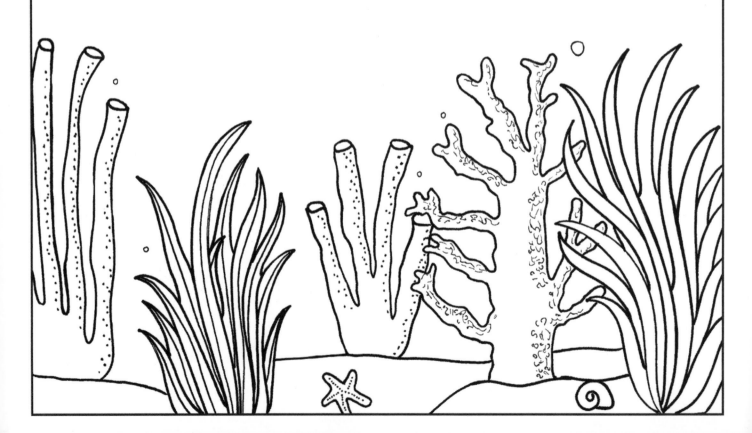

Nothing is so strong as gentleness,

nothing so gentle as real strength.

—SAINT FRANCIS DE SALES

In all things of nature

there is something of the marvelous.

—ARISTOTLE

A leopard does not change his spots,

or change his feeling that spots are rather a credit.

—IVY COMPTON-BURNETT

To fly we have to have resistance.

—MAYA LIN

Live in the sunshine,

swim the sea, drink the wild air.

—RALPH WALDO EMERSON

Be faithful in small things because it is

in them that your strength lies.

—MOTHER TERESA

A dog is the only thing on earth

that loves you more than

he loves himself.

—JOSH BILLINGS

The sea, once it casts its spell,

holds one in its net of wonder forever.

—JACQUES-YVES COUSTEAU

There are no lines in nature,

only areas of colour, one against another.

—EDWARD MANET